Primeros Sonidos

Isabel e Iván

Cathy Camarena, M.Ed., and Gloria B. Ruff, M.Ed.

Consulting Editors
Lourdes Flores-Hanson, M.S.E., and Gloria Rosso-White

ABDO
Publishing Company

Published by ABDO Publishing Company, 4940 Viking Drive, Edina, Minnesota 55435.

Printed in the United States.

Credits
Curriculum Coordinator: Nancy Tuminelly
Cover and Interior Design and Production: Mighty Media
Child Photography: Steven Wewerka, Wewerka Photography
Photo Credits: AbleStock, Brand X Pictures, Comstock, Photodisc

Library of Congress Cataloging-in-Publication Data

Camarena, Cathy, 1966-
Isabel e Iván / Cathy Camarena, Gloria B. Ruff.
p. cm. -- (Primeros sonidos)
ISBN 1-59679-875-0 (hardcover)
ISBN 1-59679-876-9 (paperback)
1. Spanish language--Consonants--Juvenile literature. I. Ruff, Gloria B., 1971-
II. Title. III. Series.

PC4159.C6576 2006
468.1'3--dc22

2005056905

SandCastle™ books are created by a professional team of educators, reading specialists, and content developers around five essential components that include phonemic awareness, phonics, vocabulary, text comprehension, and fluency. All books are written, reviewed, and leveled for guided and early intervention reading, and designed for use in shared, guided, and independent reading and writing activities to support a balanced approach to literacy instruction.

Let Us Know

After reading the book, SandCastle would like you to tell us your stories about reading. What is your favorite page? Was there something hard that you needed help with? Share the ups and downs of learning to read. We want to hear from you! To get posted on the ABDO Publishing Company Web site, send us e-mail at:

sandcastle@abdopub.com

SandCastle Level: Beginning

Ii

A B C Ch D E F G H

I J K L Ll M N Ñ O P

Q R S T U V W X Y Z

a b c ch d e f g h

i j k l ll m n ñ o p

q r s t u v w x y z

Isabel

Iván

isla

iguana

instrumentos

insectos

imán

Aquí está la .

Aquí está la  .

Aquí están los  .

Aquí están los  .

Aquí está el .

Isabel toca el instrumento.

El instrumento es un tambor.

Iván toca el insecto.
El insecto está en su dedo.

El insecto está
encima del
instrumento.

¿Cuáles de estas cosas comienzan con i?

Más palabras que comienzan con i

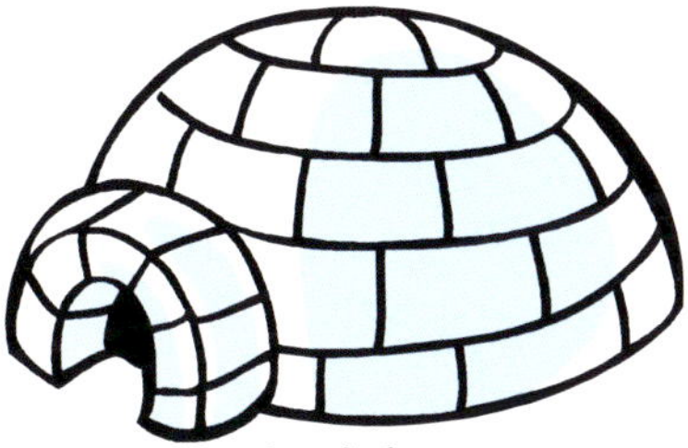

iglú

igual

impreso

impresora

invierno

About SandCastle™

A professional team of educators, reading specialists, and content developers created the SandCastle™ series to support young readers as they develop reading skills and strategies and increase their general knowledge. The SandCastle™ series has four levels that correspond to early literacy development in young children. The levels are provided to help teachers and parents select the appropriate books for young readers.

Emerging Readers
(no flags)

Beginning Readers
(1 flag)

Transitional Readers
(2 flags)

Fluent Readers
(3 flags)

These levels are meant only as a guide. All levels are subject to change.

ABDO Publishing Company

To see a complete list of SandCastle™ books and other nonfiction titles from ABDO Publishing Company, visit www.abdopub.com or contact us at:
4940 Viking Drive, Edina, Minnesota 55435 • 1-800-800-1312 • fax: 1-952-831-1632